Travel Guide To Ronda 2023

Exploring the Enchanting Beauty of Ronda: A Comprehensive Travel Guide for 2023

Scott O. Cortes

Table Of Content

INTRODUCTION

Welcome to Ronda

Welcome to Ronda, a beautiful city tucked away in the centre of Spain's Andalusian region. For those looking for an exceptional adventure, Ronda, known for its magnificent landscapes, rich history, and vibrant culture, offers an exquisite experience.

This thorough trip manual is intended to be your dependable travel companion as you discover Ronda's treasures in 2023. Everyone may find something to enjoy in Ronda, regardless of whether they are history buffs, nature lovers, foodies, or just curious travellers.

You can use the information in this book to efficiently organise your vacation. We've got you covered on everything from the best time to visit and how to get there to visa requirements and lodging choices. Additionally, you'll find insider knowledge and useful guidance to improve your vacation experience.

Learn more about Ronda's intriguing history and culture as we guide you through its historic sites, museums, and exciting festivals. Discover the famous Puente Nuevo, take in the Old Town's architectural marvels, and refresh your senses in the lovely Alameda del Tajo gardens.

Ronda has a wide range of outdoor activities for anyone looking for excitement. Explore the Sierra de las Nieves Natural Park, go hiking on gorgeous routes, or go rock climbing and caving for an adrenaline rush.

Without sampling Ronda's mouthwatering cuisine, no travelogue about the city would be complete. Enjoy authentic Andalusian cuisine, become engrossed in the vibrant tapas scene, and explore the area's renowned wines.

We've included ideas for thrilling day trips to neighbouring sights, such as the gorgeous White Villages, the historic city of Acinipo, and the breathtaking Grazalema Natural Park, if you want to extend your discovery beyond Ronda.

To ensure a smooth and pleasurable journey, you can discover important information on money, transportation, safety advice, and helpful resources in the practical information section.

We hope that this guide will motivate you to travel to Ronda and experience its alluring beauty, fascinating history, and welcoming people. Prepare to discover this interesting location in 2023 and make memories that will last a lifetime.

Why Visit Ronda in 2023

In 2023, there are several compelling reasons to travel to Ronda. To name a few:

- **Beautiful Landscapes**: Ronda is recognized for its stunning scenery and charming ambiance. Ronda is a visual feast that will leave you in amazement, from its imposing cliffs and narrow valleys to the breathtaking views of the nearby countryside.

- **Rich Historical Background:** Ronda has a long and fascinating history. It is one of the oldest towns in Spain and is dotted with historic sites, well-preserved Moorish buildings, and ancient ruins that offer an insight into its illustrious history. Discover the ruins of Roman towns, meander through the Old Town's narrow lanes, and take in the stunning Puente Nuevo, a famous bridge that crosses the El Tajo Gorge.

- **Cultural Heritage:** Get to know the friendly and welcoming people of Ronda by immersing yourself in its colourful culture. The city is well-known for its annual celebrations, such the Feria de Pedro Romero, where you can catch exciting flamenco shows, customary bullfights, and vibrant parades. To learn more about the area's creative and cultural past, explore the nearby museums and art galleries.

- **Outdoor Adventures:** If you enjoy being outside, Ronda has a variety of activities to suit your sense of adventure. Ride a horse through the nearby hills, explore bicycle routes that wind through lovely scenery, or hike along scenic trails that lead to stunning overlooks. The Sierra de las Nieves Natural Park is close by, so Ronda offers opportunities for environment lovers to explore several ecosystems and see uncommon creatures.

- Ronda is a gourmet paradise, offering a delicious selection of authentic Andalusian cuisine. Enjoy tapas and regional delicacies including paella, gazpacho, and the renowned serrano ham. Because Ronda is known for its vineyards and winemaking culture, pair your meals with regional wines.

- A true Andalusian experience may be had in Ronda, which offers a glimpse into the culture and way of life of the region. You may immerse yourself in the local way of life away from the hectic tourist hordes, wander through the lovely streets, connect with friendly residents, and experience a leisurely pace of living that captures the spirit of southern Spain.

- **Accessibility**: Ronda is a convenient place to visit because it is easily accessible. It has good rail and road connections, with frequent bus and railway service from Spain's largest cities. Its central Andalusia position also makes it a convenient base for exploring adjacent cities and attractions, giving it the perfect starting point for more adventures.

Ronda in 2023 offers a captivating location that ensures an unforgettable holiday experience, whether you're looking for history, natural beauty, cultural experiences, or simply a calm getaway.

How to Use this Guide

Here are some suggestions on how to utilise this trip guide to Ronda in 2023 to its most potential:

- **Check out the introduction**: Read the introduction section first for a summary of what to expect in the rest of the guide. It will describe the main characteristics of Ronda, the aim of the manual, and provide instructions on how to use the material.

- **Plan Your vacation**: If you're arranging a vacation to Ronda, start by reading the "Planning Your Trip to Ronda" chapter. You may learn more about the ideal time to go, transportation alternatives, visa requirements, and lodging options in this area. To plan an effective trip, take your preferences, spending capacity, and time constraints into account.

- **Examine the Chapters**: The guide is broken up into a number of sections that explore various facets of Ronda. Every chapter specialises in one subject, such as history and culture, top sights, outdoor activities, gastronomy, day trips, and useful information. Examine the chapters that relate to your interests and objectives for your trip to Ronda.

- **Consult Maps:** To help you understand the locations of attractions, landmarks, and suggested routes, the guide may include maps. Utilise these maps to organise your itinerary, comprehend the layout of the city, and make it simpler to move around Ronda.

- Throughout the guide, you'll find helpful hints and information that will make your trip more enjoyable. These sections may include information about regional customs, modes of transportation, safety advice, helpful websites, and suggested resources. To make sure that your trip is easygoing and enjoyable, pay attention to this advice.

- **Make a Checklist:** As you read the guide, make a note of the sights, things to do, and experiences that you find appealing. To remember the places you want to go, the eateries you want to sample, and the festivals or events you want to go to, make a list or an itinerary. You may make the most of your stay in Ronda by doing this.

- Remember that this advice is just a starting point and that you can personalise your stay in Ronda to suit your tastes. Make use of the information as a starting point and don't be afraid to delve deeper than what is suggested. To make your visit to Ronda special and unforgettable, seek out hidden jewels, engage with the locals, and welcome spontaneous moments.

By properly utilising this guide, you may arrange a well-rounded trip to Ronda in 2023, make wise decisions, and get the most out of this magical city. Travel safely!

PLANNING YOUR TRIP TO RONDA

Best Time to Visit

Depending on your choices and the experiences you're looking for, there is no one optimum time to visit Ronda. When deciding on the best time for your vacation, take into account the following factors:

- **Weather:** The Mediterranean environment that Ronda receives is known for its moderate winters and hot summers. Generally speaking, the spring (April to June) and fall (September to November) months offer comfortable temperatures, making them popular travel times.

  The spring season delivers blooming flowers and lush green scenery, while the autumn season displays colourful foliage. If you can tolerate the heat, the summers can still be a wonderful season to travel because temperatures tend to peak in July and August.

- **Crowds**: During the summer, particularly in July and August, when tourists swarm to the city, Ronda is typically busiest. Consider going during the shoulder seasons of spring and autumn if you like to avoid enormous crowds and lengthy lines. The mood will be more laid-back, and your chances of finding lodging and activities with less visitors will be better.

- **Festivals and Events:** Throughout the year, Ronda holds a number of festivals and cultural events, which give the city a vivacious spirit. Consider organising your trip around these events if you want to fully experience the local culture. One of the most well-known events is the Feria de Pedro Romero, which typically takes place in early September and features traditional bullfighting, flamenco performances, and vibrant parades.

- **Outside Activities**: The spring and autumn months are typically more ideal due to the cooler temperatures if you enjoy outside adventures and activities like hiking, cycling, or horseback riding.

  While autumn gives gorgeous foliage and milder temps for enjoying Ronda's natural surroundings, spring offers blooming wildflowers and nice weather.

- **Budget**: Depending on the season, the cost of lodging and travel may change. Major holidays in the height of the summer season are typically more expensive. To possibly save money on hotels and airfares, think about travelling during off-peak times.

In conclusion, the spring (April to June) and fall (September to November) seasons are the best times to visit Ronda since the weather is good, crowds are often lower, and outdoor activities may be comfortably enjoyed.

However, going in the summer can also be an option if you can take the heat and are keen on taking in the vibrant environment or going to certain events. In the end, pick a period that fits your tastes and interests for an unforgettable trip to Ronda.

Getting to Ronda

Due to the city's excellent transit connections, getting to Ronda is comparatively simple. Here are the main methods for contacting Ronda:

- **By Air:** Malaga Airport (AGP), which is about 62 miles (100 kilometres) from Ronda, is the closest significant airport. A lot of flights from significant cities in Europe and other areas of the world arrive at this international airport. You can travel to Ronda from the airport by:

- **Bus**: The Malaga Airport and Ronda are connected by frequent bus services. Buses are cosy and air-conditioned, and the trip takes around two hours. To guarantee availability, check the bus timetables and buy tickets in advance.

- If you prefer the flexibility of driving, renting a car from Malaga Airport is a convenient alternative. The AP-7 and A-397 highways take about 1.5 to 2 hours to get to Ronda, and there are several car rental agencies with desks there.

- **By Train:** Ronda has a train station in the heart of the city, making travel by rail possible. However, take aware that the high-speed AVE train network is not accessible from Ronda's train station.

In order to get a regional train or bus to Ronda, you usually need to first take a train to a nearby city, such as Malaga or Seville. Spain's trains are dependable, comfortable, and provide beautiful views of the countryside.

- **By Bus:** Ronda has excellent bus service that connects it to other Spanish cities. Buses connect with large towns including Malaga, Seville, Granada, and Cordoba to Ronda. With spacious coaches and several daily departures, using the bus is a simple and economical option.

  Check the schedules and purchase tickets well in advance, particularly during the busiest travel times.

- **By Car:** Ronda is easily reachable by road, and a car gives you the freedom to explore the area in which it is located. Major highways link Ronda to neighbouring cities and popular tourist locations. Roads A-374 and A-397 are frequently used to travel to Ronda by automobile. Depending on where you start, the trip's duration may change, so make sure to account for traffic conditions when making your plans.

- Public transportation, taxis, and walking are practical ways to get around Ronda and discover its attractions after you arrive. Because of its relative compactness, the city centre is simple to tour on foot.

When selecting a method of transportation to get to Ronda, keep in mind to check the most recent timetables, purchase tickets in advance if at all feasible, and take your preferences and budget into account. Travel safely!

Visa requirements and Travel Documents

Depending on your country, your intended purpose for visiting Ronda, Spain, and the length of your stay, you may need a visa. The following general information on Ronda visa requirements and travel documentation is provided:

- Spain, a member of the Schengen Area, is where Ronda is situated. You must obtain a Schengen visa in advance of visiting Ronda if you are a citizen of a nation that is not excluded from the requirement. With this visa, you are able to visit and remain in Ronda and other Schengen nations for up to 90 days out of every 180 days.

- **Visa Exemptions**: For brief visits, citizens of a few countries may not need a Schengen visa. Depending on the bilateral agreements between nations, these exemptions change. If you are a citizen of a nation with whom the Schengen Area has a visa exemption agreement, you do not need to obtain a visa in order to enter Ronda and remain there for up to 90 days inside of a 180-day window. Prior to travelling, it is crucial to confirm the precise visa requirements based on your nationality.

- **Validity of Passport**: Ensure that your passport is valid for at least three months after the date you intend to travel from Ronda. This is a standard prerequisite for the majority of foreigners entering Spain. To prevent any travel issues, it is usually essential to have a valid passport with enough remaining time on it.

- **Supporting Documents**: You will typically need to submit supporting documents when applying for a Schengen visa, including a filled-out visa application form, a current passport, recent passport-sized photos, travel insurance, proof of lodging in Ronda, round-trip airline tickets, evidence of your ability to pay for your stay, and a detailed itinerary.

- If you need a Schengen visa, you must apply at the Spanish embassy or consulate in your country of origin or where you are now residing. The application procedure can involve turning in the necessary paperwork, paying the visa fee, and showing up in person for a biometric data collecting session.

- For the most recent and correct information on visa requirements and the application process, it is crucial to visit the official website of the Spanish embassy or consulate in your country or the embassy/consulate that represents Spain. It's crucial to confirm the most recent laws well in advance of your intended travel as visa requirements are subject to change.

Please be aware that this material only serves as a general outline, and that exact criteria might change depending on your unique situation. It is always advised to get individualised and current visa information before visiting Ronda from the necessary authorities or a reputable visa firm.

Accommodation Options

Ronda provides a selection of lodging choices to fit different needs and interests. You can discover accommodations to suit your preferences, whether you're looking for opulent hotels, lovely boutique lodgings, budget-friendly hostels, or classic guesthouses.

Here are a few popular places to stay in Ronda:

- **Hotels**: Ronda has many lodging options that can be found in a range of price ranges and offer a comfortable stay. You can find luxury hotels with first-rate features like spas, swimming pools, and sweeping views of the city and its surroundings. Additionally, there are mid-priced and low-cost hotels that provide cosy lodgings and handy locations in the city.

- **Paradores**: Paradores are state-run luxury hotels that are frequently located in old castles, palatial homes, and monastic structures. A Parador hotel in Ronda, Spain, is housed in a former town hall and offers a distinctive and opulent experience with stunning views of the El Tajo Gorge.

- **Hotel Boutiques**: Ronda is renowned for its quaint hotel boutiques that offer a bespoke and intimate setting. The distinctive decor, chic interiors, and attentive service of these boutique hotels frequently make for an unforgettable stay with a dash of regional flavour.

- **Guesthouses and Bed & Breakfasts:** Ronda has a selection of guesthouses and

B&Bs, particularly in the city's historic district. These businesses frequently offer comfortable accommodations, attentive service, and a pleasant atmosphere. An intimate encounter and an opportunity to speak with welcoming hosts can be had by staying in a guesthouse or bed and breakfast.

- **Hostels**: Ronda offers a few hostels that offer private or dorm-style rooms if you're on a tight budget or prefer a more communal setting. For backpackers, lone travellers, or those wishing to connect with other travellers and swap stories, hostels are a fantastic choice.

- **Rural lodging**: If you want to experience the calm and tranquillity of the countryside, think about staying in a rural lodging outside of Ronda. These might be country homes, outlying lodges, or farm stays that let you take in the scenery and the tranquil atmosphere of the Andalusian countryside.

- Think about things like location, accessibility to attractions, facilities, reviews, and cost when selecting your lodging. It is essential to reserve your lodging in advance to ensure availability and lock in the best rates, especially during the busiest travel times, festivals, or holidays.

A thorough list of lodging alternatives in Ronda may be found on well-known online travel booking companies and hotel websites, together with user reviews and ratings to aid in decision-making.

Essential Travel Tips

Plan your trip and do your homework about Ronda's tourist sites, regional traditions, travel alternatives, and weather before you go. Making the most of your vacation will depend on you having a basic familiarity of the city.

- **Best Time to Visit**: Based on your choices, think about the ideal time to visit Ronda. Consider the weather, the number of people, and any particular events or festivals you might wish to attend.

- Drink plenty of water because Ronda can get very hot, especially in the summer. Carry a water bottle with you and sip on lots of liquids all day to stay hydrated.

- Wear shoes that are comfortable because the city centre of Ronda has winding, mountainous streets. To easily explore the city, use comfy shoes like sneakers or walking shoes.

- **Respect Local Customs**: Get to know the traditions and customs of Ronda and Spain as a whole. Respect local customs, observe any etiquette rules, and dress modestly when visiting places of worship.

- **Cash & Currency:** Keep some cash on hand for modest transactions since certain businesses might not accept cards or have minimum purchase requirements. In Ronda, there are ATMs where you can get cash when you need it.

- **Security and safety:** Ronda is a generally safe city, but it's always a good idea to be on the lookout for danger and take the necessary precautions. Follow common sense safety precautions such as keeping an eye on your things and avoiding nighttime solo strolling in dimly lit places.

- Consider purchasing travel insurance that includes coverage for medical costs, trip cancellation, and loss or theft of personal items. It's always preferable to be ready for unforeseen circumstances.

- Although English is widely spoken by residents in tourist areas, Ronda's primary language is Spanish. To make conversation easier and to demonstrate respect for the local way of life, it is beneficial to learn a few fundamental Spanish words and phrases.

- **Try the local cuisine**: Ronda has a thriving food scene. Eat and drink your way through typical Andalusian fare like tapas, gazpacho, paella, and regional wines. Don't be afraid to investigate neighbourhood restaurants and sample local cuisine.

- **Consider Venturing Off the Beaten Path:** While Ronda's famous sights like the Puente Nuevo bridge and the Bullring are must-see destinations, consider exploring beyond the main attractions. To find hidden jewels, explore the winding alleyways, go to lesser-known locations, and immerse yourself in the community.

- **Make Memories:** Ronda is a beautiful city, so be sure to pack your camera or smartphone to record the breathtaking scenery, elaborate architecture, and memorable experiences while you're there.

Before leaving for Ronda, don't forget to check for any travel warnings or instructions given by the local government or the embassy or consulate of your home country. This charming Spanish city can be visited with ease and enjoyment by following these travel advice..

EXPLORING RONDA'S HISTORY AND CULTURE

A Glimpse into Ronda's Past

A magnificent tapestry of cultures and civilizations has been left behind by the extensive history of Ronda over thousands of years. Here's a look at Ronda's earlier:

- **Prehistoric Period:** There is evidence of prehistoric human occupation in the region surrounding Ronda. The presence of early settlers in the area is evidenced by cave paintings and archaeological sites.

- **Roman Era:** Ronda, then known as Arunda, was a significant Roman city. Along the Via Augusta, a crucial Roman route linking Cadiz and Rome, it served as a vital outpost. The streets' design and the remains of a long-gone bridge both reflect the city's Roman past.

- **Islamic sovereignty**: When the Moors conquered the Iberian Peninsula in the eighth century, Ronda came under Islamic sovereignty. Due to its advantageous location atop a hill, the city developed into a significant fortress. Ronda prospered as a centre of culture and learning throughout this time, leaving behind stunning structures like the Old Bridge and the Arab Baths.

- **Reconquista and Christian Rule**: During the Reconquista in 1485, Ronda was taken by the Catholic monarchs Ferdinand and Isabella. Alongside the already-existing Islamic structures, Christian buildings, like churches and monasteries, were built in the city.

- **Banditry and Romanticism:** In the 18th and 19th centuries, Ronda developed a reputation for banditry, and stories of bandits' exploits captured the imagination of Romantic authors and artists. The area was home to the infamous bandit El Tempranillo.

- Ronda was an important player in the Spanish Civil War (1936–1939) throughout the modern era. Due to the division of the city into two factions, there was fierce fighting and widespread destruction. Ronda has been magnificently renovated today, embracing modern development while maintaining its traditional charm.

- Ronda has been a source of inspiration for many writers, thinkers, and artists throughout history. Famous people including Ernest Hemingway, Rainer Maria Rilke, and Orson Welles were inspired by it because of its stunning scenery and fascination for romance.

The layers of history that have defined Ronda's character can be appreciated by visitors by immersing themselves in the city's past. Ronda offers a fascinating trip through history, taking in everything from Islamic architectural marvels to pre-Christian relics and old Roman ruins.

Historical Landmarks and Monuments

The historical landmarks and monuments of Ronda are well-known, and each one highlights a distinct facet of the city's rich legacy. Here are some noteworthy locations to visit:

- **The Puente Nuevo (New Bridge),** a majestic bridge that crosses the El Tajo Gorge and links the old and new parts of the city, is arguably Ronda's most recognizable landmark. The 18th-century bridge, a landmark of Ronda, provides stunning panoramic views.

- **The Puente Viejo**, sometimes referred to as the Arab Bridge, is a historic stone bridge that existed before the Puente Nuevo. It affords a lovely perspective of the surrounding landscape and offers a window into Ronda's Islamic heritage.

- **Mondragon Palace:** The Mondragon Palace is a magnificent example of Moorish architecture and is close to the Puente Nuevo. It contains the Ronda Municipal Museum, which showcases relics from antiquity and sheds light on the city's past.

- **Alameda del Tajo**: This lovely park, which is located on the edge of the El Tajo Gorge, provides breathtaking views of the surrounding landscape and cliffs. It's the perfect place to unwind, stroll lazily, or have a picnic.

- The historic home known as Casa del Rey Moro (House of the Moorish King) is linked to Ronda's Moorish origins. Visitors can stroll through its gardens, enter the

Water Mine, and find the gorge's secret passageways.

- **Arab Baths:** The 13th-century Arab Baths in Ronda offer a look into the Moorish bathing tradition. The well-preserved ruins display the period's architectural design and bathing customs.

- In the centre of Ronda's historic district stands the beautiful Church of Santa Maria la Mayor. It was built in the 13th century, and its architecture blends Gothic, Renaissance, and Baroque styles.

- The Plaza de Toros is one of the oldest and most recognizable bullrings in all of Spain. Ronda is known for its bullfighting heritage. To understand the cultural relevance of bullfighting in the area, it is worthwhile to travel there.

- The Casa de Don Bosco historical house museum provides a look into upper-class daily life in Ronda in the 18th century. It displays vintage home objects, artwork, and furniture and offers a fascinating look into the city's past.

These are only a few of the historical sites and monuments that Ronda has to offer tourists. You can immerse yourself in the city's past and enjoy its architectural and cultural heritage by visiting these locations.

Museums and Art Galleries

A fuller understanding of the history, culture, and aesthetic heritage of Ronda can be gained from the city's numerous museums and art galleries. Here are some noteworthy galleries and museums to visit:

- The Museo Lara houses a sizable collection of antiques and oddities and is housed in a gorgeously renovated 18th-century palace. It offers a fascinating voyage through history with displays on archaeology, clocks, weapons, vintage cars, and more.

- **Museo Municipal de Ronda:** Located inside the Mondragon Palace, the Municipal Museum of Ronda exhibits Roman and Moorish antiquities from antiquity. The museum also features historical records, artwork, and offers historical perspectives on the city.

- The Casa del Rey Moro Museum is housed inside the Casa del Rey Moro, also known as the House of the Moorish King. It provides a window into the house's design as well as Ronda's Moorish past.

  Visitors can stroll around the gardens, take in the antiquities, and enter the historic water system known as the Water Mine.

- **Joaquin Peinado Museum:** Dedicated to the creations of the eminent Ronda-born artist Joaqun Peinado, this museum displays his ceramics, sculptures, paintings, and sketches. The group of works displays Peinados development as an artist and his impact on Spanish art.

- **Unicaja Museum Joaqun Peinado**: Another museum devoted to the artist features a greater selection of his creations and investigates the cultural environment in which they were created. Temporary exhibits and cultural activities are held in the museum.

- **Puente Nuevo Interpretation Centre:** This centre offers information about the development of Ronda's renowned bridge and is close to the Puente Nuevo. Educative exhibitions and interactive displays help visitors comprehend the importance of the bridge better.

- **Contemporary Art Museum of Ronda:** Featuring works by regional and international artists, this museum specialises in contemporary art. There are several different modern art mediums on display, such as paintings, sculptures, photographs, and installations.

- **Galera de Arte Pedro Lobato Hoyos:** Situated in the ancient town, this art gallery displays ceramics, paintings, and sculptures made by regional and national artists. The gallery gives artists a place to display their works.

- Temporary art exhibitions and cultural activities are held in La Casa del Gigante. It supports regional artists and provides a venue for the display of their creations, which may include mixed media, photography, and paintings.

From ancient items and archaeological displays to modern artworks, Ronda's museums and art galleries provide a wide variety of cultural experiences. A fuller understanding of Ronda's cultural heritage and artistic accomplishments can be gained through exploring them.

Local Traditions and Festivals

The city of Ronda is steeped in tradition and holds a number of vibrant events throughout the year. The lively culture and heritage of the area are celebrated at these events. These prominent Ronda customs and celebrations are listed below:

- The most important and enduring event of Ronda is the Feria de Pedro Romero, which takes place every year in the first few days of September. The festival, which bears Pedro Romero's name in honour of a well-known local bullfighter, includes bullfights, flamenco dances, parades, live music, and traditional attire.

  The city comes to life during festive events that draw both residents and tourists.

- Like many Spanish cities, Ronda observes Semana Santa (Holy Week) with solemn rituals and religious processions during the week preceding Easter Sunday. Religious statues that have been elaborately decorated are paraded through the streets, escorted by marching bands and penitents wearing traditional garb.

- **Romera de la Virgen de la Cabeza:** In May, Ronda conducts a pilgrimage in honour of the town 's patron saint, the Romera de la Virgen de la Cabeza. A procession of people wearing traditional garb leaves the city and travels through the countryside to the Sanctuary of Virgen de la Cabeza. It is a happy celebration with music, dance, and local cuisine.

- **Ronda's Wine Festival:** Held in May, this event honours the top-notch wines produced in the area. Ronda-area wineries display their goods while providing wine tastings, culinary pairings, and educational events. It's a wonderful chance to taste regional wines and see how wine is made.

- **Corpus Christi:** The "cabezudos" parade, when participants parade while donning enormous papier-mâché heads, is a part of the Corpus Christi celebration in Ronda. On the streets, elaborate floral carpets with intricate designs are also produced.

- **Feria Goyesca**: The Feria Goyesca is a special occasion that takes place at the Feria de Pedro Romero and is inspired by Francisco de Goya's artwork. Participants recreate the atmosphere of Goya's time by dressing in classic 18th-century costume. The matadors who perform the bullfights during this festival dress in outfits that are reminiscent of Goya's paintings.

- **Feria de San Francisco**: Held in the first few days of October, this festival honours Ronda's patron saint. Horse parades, traditional dances, musical performances, and other cultural events are all part of the celebration. It's a fun occasion that unites the neighbourhood.

These celebrations and customs offer a window into Ronda's rich cultural diversity. Visitors can get a firsthand impression of the city's vibrant spirit, traditions, and regional customs by taking part in or seeing these festivals.

RONDA'S TOP ATTRACTIONS

The Puente Nuevo: Iconic Bridge of Ronda

The New Bridge, commonly known as the Puente Nuevo, is without a doubt Ronda's most recognizable feature. This wonderful bridge connects the historic and modern sections of the city across the breathtaking El Tajo Gorge.

Let's examine the Puente Nuevo and its significance in more detail:

- **Construction and Design**: Work on the Puente Nuevo's construction started in 1751 and took more than 40 years to finish. José Martn de Aldehuela, an architect famous for his knowledge of bridge engineering, created the bridge. Neoclassical and

Renaissance influences can be seen in its architecture.

- The Puente Nuevo has come to represent Ronda and serve as a reminder of the city's engineering expertise. Its construction was a great achievement because it crosses a gorge that drops 120 metres (390 feet) below.

- **Breathtaking Panorama Views**: The Guadalevin River, El Tajo Gorge, and the scenic surroundings of Ronda are all visible from the bridge. From numerous vantage points along the bridge, visitors may take in the craggy cliffs, the rich flora, and the sheer size of the valley.

- An interpretive centre is located at the southern end of the bridge, where guests may find out more about the Puente Nuevo's construction, significance, and history. The centre offers educational exhibits, displays, and audiovisual presentations that give visitors a better appreciation of the engineering marvel that is the bridge.

- **Photography and filming**: The Puente Nuevo is a well-liked subject for photographers and filmmakers due to its dramatic surroundings and stunning architecture. Its magnificence against the gorge's backdrop offers a stunning visual spectacle that captures the interest of both artists and tourists.

- The Puente Nuevo had a significant historical impact on Ronda, especially during the Spanish Civil War. Between Nationalist and Republican forces, there was fierce fighting there, and the bridge came to represent resistance. It still stands as proof of Ronda's tenacity and power today.

- **Cultural Events:** Throughout the year, the Puente Nuevo serves as a location for a number of cultural celebrations and events. Concerts, traditional performances, and even the occasional bullfight are among the events that take place here and offer a singular and fascinating experience.

You may admire Ronda's architectural wonder and natural splendour by going to Puente Nuevo. The bridge is a must-see site that captures the spirit and grandeur of the city because of its imposing presence and the breathtaking vistas it provides.

The Bullring: Plaza de Toros

One of Ronda's most well-known sights, the Plaza de Toros, or Bullring, is renowned for both its historical importance and its exquisite architectural design. What you should know about the Plaza de Toros is as follows:

- The Plaza de Toros is one of the oldest bullrings in Spain and has a vital role in the bullfighting culture of the nation. It was constructed in 1785, which makes it older than many other bullrings. It is a significant cultural and historical site.

- Unlike other bullrings, which are oval in shape, the Plaza de Toros in Ronda has a distinctive circular shape. This design, which has since become a defining characteristic of Spanish bullrings, was initially used in a purpose-built bullring.

- **Goyesca Festival and Pedro Romero:** Pedro Romero, a renowned bullfighter from Ronda who revolutionised the sport in the 18th century, is strongly linked to the Plaza de Toros. The Goyesca Festival, named for the Spanish painter Francisco de Goya, is held annually at the bullring.

  Bullfighters dress up for this festival in classic 18th-century garb that is reminiscent of Goya's paintings, creating a singular and breathtaking spectacle.

- The bullring is home to a museum with exhibits that explore the tradition and history of bullfighting. The mementos and antiques related to Ronda's bullfighting are displayed in exhibits. The significance, history, and traditions of this contentious sport are all available for visitors to learn about.

- **Views and architecture:** The Plaza de Toros has a stunning neoclassical façade and a stately entrance. Visitors are welcome to tour the church, bullfighting ring, and seating area within. Ronda and the surrounding countryside are visible from the top of the bullring, providing magnificent photo opportunities.

- **Cultural Events**: In addition to bullfights, the Plaza de Toros organises a number of cultural occasions all through the year, including plays, concerts, and traditional celebrations. Visitors get the opportunity to experience Ronda's energetic atmosphere and rich cultural legacy through these events.

- **Guided Tours:** For those who are interested in learning more about the background and significance of the Plaza de Toros, guided tours are available. Experienced tour guides give thorough explanations of the bullring's structure, bullfighting customs, and place in Ronda's cultural history.

The Plaza de Toros is a fascinating attraction that offers insights into Spain's cultural legacy, whether or not you are interested in bullfighting. The beauty of its architecture, historical importance, and cultural activities make it a must-see location when in Ronda.

The Old Town:La Ciudad

La Ciudad, or the Old Town, is a picturesque and significant area in Ronda that perfectly captures the character of the entire city. The Old Town offers a beautiful fusion of history, culture, and picturesque beauty with its winding streets, whitewashed homes, and intriguing architecture. In Ronda's Old Town, you can explore the following:

- **Puente Nuevo:** The renowned Puente Nuevo, the New Bridge that crosses the El Tajo Gorge, is located in the Old Town. Crossing this breath-inspiring bridge and taking in the amazing vistas it offers is a great place to start your journey.

- **Plaza de Espana**: Situated close to the Puente Nuevo, Plaza de Espana is a busy square encircled by grand old houses and buzzing eateries. It's a terrific place to unwind, observe people, and take in Ronda's energetic environment.

- **Calle de la Bola**: Calle de la Bola, one of the main streets of the Old Town, is dotted with boutiques, eateries, and historic buildings. Take a stroll down this charming street, peruse the shops, and savour some regional cuisine.

- Explore the Casa del Rey Moro, also known as the House of the Moorish King, to learn more about Ronda's Moorish past. Wander through the lovely gardens as you descend into the Water Mine, a set of steep steps carved out of the valley.

- Visit the Santa Maria la Mayor Church, a magnificent Gothic building that serves as a reminder of Ronda's rich religious history.

Take at the magnificent exterior details of the church and then go inside to be amazed.

- **Plaza Duquesa de Parcent**: This picturesque square, encircled by ancient structures and vibrant eateries, is the centre of activity in the Old Town. It's the ideal spot for a break, a cup of coffee, and to take in the atmosphere.

- **Arab Baths (Banos Arabes):** Learn about Ronda's Moorish heritage at the Arab Baths, a beautifully preserved building that provides insights into the Moors' bathing customs. Admire the architectural intricacies as you stroll through the eerie rooms.

- Museo Lara, Museo Municipal de Ronda, and Casa del Gigante are just a few of the museums and art galleries that can be found in the

Old Town. The history, art, and oddities of Ronda are better understood thanks to these cultural institutions.

- **Squares & secret Corners**: As you stroll through the Old Town's winding streets, you'll come across small squares, gorgeous passageways, and secret corners. Explore these lesser-known locations so you can uncover hidden treasures and take striking pictures.

- **Local Cuisine:** Traditional taverns and restaurants can be found all over the Old Town, giving visitors a chance to experience Andalusian cuisine's true flavours. Taste some tapas, sip some regional wine, and savour Ronda's delectable cuisine.

The Old Town of Ronda welcomes you to explore, discover, and take in the timeless appeal of this intriguing city with its rich history, spectacular architecture, and lively environment.

Arab Baths: Baños Árabes

A remarkable historical site in Ronda that provides a look into the Moorish past of the city are the Arab Baths, also known as Baos Arabes. What you should know about the Baos Arabs is as follows:

- The Baos Arabes date back to the 13th century, when Ronda was governed by the Moors. They were an essential component of Moorish everyday life and hygiene customs, demonstrating the period's great engineering and architectural abilities.

- **Architectural Grace**: The Banos Arabes exhibit the characteristic Moorish bath house design. The baths showcase the superb craftsmanship and meticulous attention to detail that distinguished Moorish architecture with their horseshoe arches, finely carved stucco work, and geometric patterns.

- **Layout and Design:** The baths are separated into many areas, each of which has a distinct function. These areas consist of the changing rooms, frigidarium (cold room), tepidarium (warm room), and caldarium (hot room). The architecture and design were carefully thought out to offer a soothing and revitalising bathing experience.

- **Elements of the Baths**: The Baos rabes have a number of components that were essential to the Moors' bathing practices. The heating system that pumped warm air through the walls and under the flooring, as well as the central pool that was used for immersion and purification, are some examples.

- When you enter the Baos Arabes, you are immediately enveloped in a calm and serene ambiance. You can envision the past and the experiences of those who once used these baths thanks to the quiet lighting, cold temperature, and elaborate architectural elements that create a tranquil atmosphere.

- **Historical Significance**: The Baos Arabes are a visible reminder of the diverse cultures that have shaped Ronda throughout its history. They provide as evidence of the creativity and elegance of Moorish civilization, which profoundly influenced Ronda's built environment.

- **Cultural Interpretation:** The Baos Arabes are now a historical and cultural site where tourists may learn about the influence of the Moors on Ronda. The significance of the baths, the bathing customs, and the broader backdrop of Moorish culture in the area are explained by interpretive panels and guided tours.

- **Preservation and restoration**: To secure their preservation and to maintain their architectural integrity, the Baos Arabes underwent considerable restoration. Visitors may now see the baths in all of their former glory and understand its historical and cultural significance thanks to the restoration work.

The Baos Arabes in Ronda provide a singular chance to travel back in time and discover the intriguing world of Moorish bathing customs. It is a remarkable experience that displays the city's multicultural diversity thanks to the eerie environment, exquisite architecture, and historical insights.

Alameda del Tajo: Ronda's Beautiful Gardens

Ronda's Alameda del Tajo is a lovely oasis that provides a tranquil escape from the busy city streets. What you should know about this lovely green area is as follows:

- **Location and Scenic Views:** Alameda del Tajo offers breathtaking panoramic views of the surrounding countryside, the Puente Nuevo, and the Guadalevin River. It is located on the edge of the El Tajo Gorge. It's the perfect location for admiring Ronda's magnificent scenery and getting priceless photos.

- Alameda del Tajo's gardens are home to a wide variety of plant species, including trees, flowers, and shrubs. As you stroll down the walkways, you'll pass vibrant flowers, fragrant blossoms, and thick vegetation, which together create a calming and beautiful ambience.

- The Fountain of Eight Spouts, also known as the Fuente de los Ocho Caos, is located in the centre of Alameda del Tajo. The gardens' main focal point and added appeal is this ancient fountain that was constructed in the 17th century.

- Alameda del Tajo offers guests covered walks and chairs where they may unwind and take in the peace and quiet of nature. The gardens include plenty of places for you to relax and think, whether you're looking for shade from the heat or just want to take in the tranquil atmosphere.

- **Aviary & Birdlife**: An aviary that shelters several bird species is located in the grounds. The fascinating aspect of the garden experience is enhanced by the beautiful songs of birds as you stroll around Alameda del Tajo and take in their vivid colours.

- **Recreational Facilities**: Both locals and tourists can enjoy recreational amenities in Alameda del Tajo. It's a great place for families because there is a playground there. There are also places for picnics and leisurely strolls, enabling guests to fully take in the tranquil surroundings.

- Alameda del Tajo is the location for a number of cultural events and celebrations throughout the year. The gardens offer a stunning environment for cultural festivals, bringing life and enjoyment to the Ronda neighbourhood through music concerts and outdoor shows.

- Alameda del Tajo is ideally situated close to a number of Ronda's main attractions, including the Puente Nuevo and the Old Town. It is the perfect place to begin or stop while exploring the city.

Alameda del Tajo offers a serene sanctuary where you may re-establish contact with nature, take in beautiful vistas, and sense the peace of Ronda. These lovely gardens offer a tranquil respite in the middle of the city, whether you're looking for a moment of leisure, a picturesque backdrop for photographs, or a spot to unwind with loved ones.

OUTDOOR ADVENTURES IN RONDA

Hiking and Nature Trails

Ronda is blessed with beautiful natural scenery and provides a number of hiking and nature routes that let visitors discover the region's natural splendour. Here are some well-known hiking paths and natural areas near Ronda:

- The lovely Paseo de los Molinos route follows the Guadalevin River while passing by old watermills and providing picturesque views of the surrounding area. The very simple trail is ideal for a leisurely bike ride or walk.

- The Camino de los Viajeros Románticos, or Path of Romantic Travellers, is a path that traces the routes taken by illustrious authors and artists who were moved by Ronda's beauty. The walk is a favourite among outdoor enthusiasts since it provides spectacular views of the Puente Nuevo and the surrounding scenery.

- The Sierra de Grazalema Natural Park, which is close to Ronda, is a hiking enthusiast's dream come true. It has steep canyons, rocky limestone peaks, and rich vegetation. You may explore the park's natural treasures at your own speed thanks to the many trails it offers, all of varied degrees of difficulty.

- **El Tajo Gorge:** The hike through the El Tajo Gorge itself is breathtaking. You can hike along the gorge's edge while admiring the stunning cliffs and expansive views. Visit the Mirador de Aldehuela for an incredible vantage point across the gorge.

- **La Cueva del Gato:** La Cueva del Gato (Cat's Cave), a natural wonder close to Ronda, is worth investigating. The route to the cave passes through lovely forested areas and ends in an incredible waterfall. The waterfall created a pool where you can cool yourself and swim in the clean water.

- **Hoya del Tajo:** This hike provides a distinctive viewpoint of El Tajo Gorge and Puente Nuevo. The walk leaves from the Alameda del Tajo and descends to the gorge's foot, where you can see the bridge and the soaring cliffs up close.

- The Los Molinos del Tajo route blends scenic natural areas with historic sites. It leads you along the river while passing attractive rural areas like historic mills. The trail provides peace and a look at the area's agrarian past.

- **Cueva de la Pileta:** Located a little further from Ronda, the interesting Cueva de la Pileta is famous for its ancient cave paintings. In-depth guided tours allow you to see these prehistoric works of art while taking in the surrounding natural beauty.

Remember to bring water and snacks, to respect the natural environment, and to wear appropriate footwear while starting a hiking or nature walk. The hiking paths and natural areas in Ronda provide a chance to get in touch with nature, admire the area's varied sceneries, and make priceless memories of outdoor exploration.

Exploring the Sierra de las Nieves Natural Park

Visitors who enjoy the outdoors and wildlife should explore the Sierra de las Nieves Natural Park while in Ronda.

This protected region, which is found in the province of Malaga, is renowned for its breathtaking landscapes, varied animals, and rich biodiversity. What to expect when visiting Sierra de las Nieves Natural Park is as follows:

- **Scenic Beauty:** The Sierra de las Nieves Natural Park, with its craggy mountain ranges, deep valleys, and lush woods, displays spectacular natural beauty. The park offers a broad range of landscapes that are fun to explore, from rolling hills to steep peaks.

- **Routes for Hiking:** The park offers a network of clearly marked hiking routes for hikers of all experience levels and interests. You can select trails that suit your preferences whether you're an experienced hiker or a novice. The Rio Grande Trail, Los Quejigales Trail, and Torrecilla Peak Trail are a few of the well-liked trails.

- **Wildlife**: The Sierra de las Nieves Natural Park is renowned for its diverse wildlife. Numerous plant species, such as Spanish first, Mediterranean pines, and oak woods, can be found in the park. Native creatures like mountain goats, ibex, wild boars, and many bird species can be seen by wildlife enthusiasts.

- UNESCO has classified the Sierra de las Nieves Natural Park as a Biosphere Reserve in recognition of its great ecological significance. The park's achievements in conservation and sustainable development are highlighted by this recognition.

- **La Torrecilla**: La Torrecilla, which rises to a height of 1,919 metres (6,296 feet), is the highest peak in the Sierra de las Nieves mountain range. On clear days, La Torrecilla's top offers panoramic views of the surrounding areas, including the Mediterranean Sea and the coast of Africa.

- The Botanical Garden at El Bosque is a must-see location for nature lovers and is situated inside the park. It exhibits the variety of plant species found in the Sierra de las Nieves and offers instructive details about the flora and ecosystems of the area.

- Sierra de las Nieves Natural Park contains a specialised nature interpretation centre where visitors may find out about the park's biodiversity, geology, and cultural history. The centre provides lectures, interactive displays, and exhibits to help you better comprehend the park's natural treasures.

- **Adventure Activities**: The Sierra de las Nieves Natural Park provides chances for a variety of outdoor pursuits besides hiking. You can go horseback riding, mountain biking, or go on a guided excursion to see the wildlife.

  You can participate in these activities while experiencing an exhilarating journey and the natural surroundings of the park.

Follow the park's rules, respect the environment, and leave no trace while you explore the Sierra de las Nieves

Natural Park. The park offers an amazing experience that highlights the natural wonders of the Ronda region thanks to its breathtaking scenery, profusion of species, and outdoor activities.

Cycling Routes

Bike enthusiasts may discover the gorgeous landscapes, quaint villages, and historical monuments in Ronda and the surrounding area thanks to the great bike routes that are available. Here are several noteworthy cycling routes in and around Ronda, regardless of whether you like road riding or mountain biking:

- The Ronda Loop is a well-known road cycling route that circles through a beautiful rural area and begins and concludes in Ronda. The route includes a variety of difficult climbs, exhilarating descents, and beautiful views. The distance and elevation gain can be changed according to your preferences and degree of fitness.

- **Sierra de Grazalema**: The Sierra de Grazalema Natural Park offers a variety of trails for mountain bike riders to explore.

The park features rocky landscapes, wooded regions, and picturesque mountain passes. The Puerto de las Palomas route is well-liked because it offers difficult climbs and breathtaking views.

- **Journey via the White Villages:** The White Villages of Andalusia, which include towns like Grazalema, Zahara de la Sierra, and Setenil de las Bodegas, are connected by picturesque roads and make for an unforgettable cycling journey. You'll cycle through undulating hills, olive groves, and classic white-washed villages as you become fully immersed in the area's rich cultural legacy.

- **Via Verde de la Sierra**: Cycling down this former railroad track is a special experience. From Puerto Serrano to Olvera, there is a cycling and trekking trail known as the Via Verde de la Sierra that travels through breathtaking natural settings. All ability levels can navigate the reasonably flat course.

- **Serrania de Ronda Loop**: This strenuous road cycling route traverses Serrania de Ronda, exhibiting its varied topography. You will experience magnificent views of the mountains and valleys as you travel along winding roads, through vineyards and olive orchards.

- **El Bosque Loop:** This route departs from Ronda and passes via the picturesque village of El Bosque and the surrounding countryside. The trip features peaceful surroundings, winding roads, and rolling hills. Visit El

Bosque to experience the authentic Andalusian ambiance.

- This mountain bike route from Grazalema to Zahara de la Sierra offers an exciting trip through the Sierra de Grazalema Natural Park. You'll traverse rough routes, overcome strenuous climbs, and take in breathtaking vistas of the Grazalema Mountains and the reservoir at Zahara de la Sierra.

- This road cycling route connects the charming village of Setenil de las Bodegas with the city of Ronda. You'll go by bicycle through beautiful countryside, past olive groves, and eventually reach Setenil de las Bodegas, a town renowned for its unusual dwellings that are constructed into the cliffs.

Always put safety first when cycling, and pay attention to traffic and road conditions. Check your community's laws on trail access, bike rentals, and helmet requirements. The cycling routes in Ronda provide an interesting opportunity to explore the area's natural beauty and cultural richness, whether you're a road cyclist or a mountain biker.

Horseback Riding and Equestrian Activities

The area around Ronda is ideal for equestrian activities, including horseback riding. Here are some possibilities for horseback riding in and around Ronda, regardless of your riding expertise level:

- **Horseback Riding trips**: A number of equestrian facilities and stables in the region provide escorted horseback riding trips that let you discover the stunning trails, mountains, and landscape surrounding Ronda. Knowledgeable drivers will take you along beautiful routes while imparting their knowledge of the area's past and current environment.

- Take a leisurely horseback ride in the beautiful countryside of Ronda. As you stroll along the trails, take in the peace and quiet of the vineyards, olive groves, and rolling hills. These rides provide a tranquil chance to commune with nature and experience the area's tranquil atmosphere.

- **Grazalema Natural Park:** Ride a horse through the breathtaking Sierra de Grazalema Natural Park. Take a ride across its rocky terrain, which features limestone mountains, deep valleys, and lush woods. The equestrian trails in the park offer a special viewpoint of this stunning natural setting.

- **Sunset Rides**: On a horseback ride, take in the beauty of Ronda's sunsets. Take a ride in the evening as the sun sets, bathing the surroundings in a golden glow. It's a special chance to take in Ronda's beauty at a serene and gorgeous time of day.

- **Horseback Riding classes:** Local equestrian facilities may offer horseback riding classes whether you're a beginner or wish to advance your riding abilities.

  You will be led through the fundamentals of horseback riding by knowledgeable teachers who will teach you the right methods and look out for your safety and enjoyment.

- **Equestrian Shows**: Ronda occasionally hosts equestrian competitions and events that highlight classical horsemanship techniques. These exhibits promote the Andalusian equestrian legacy through dressage, horse performances in the flamenco style, and Spanish equestrian customs. To discover whether any performances coincide with your visit, check the local events calendar.

- Excursions on horseback that last more than one day and take you across the Andalusian countryside are recommended for a more thorough experience. These guided tours offer the chance to experience various landscapes, stop by quaint communities, and spend the night in old-fashioned haciendas or rural lodgings.

It's crucial to adhere to your instructor or guide's instructions, wear the proper riding gear, and treat the horses with kindness and respect when taking part in horseback riding activities. Horseback riding in Ronda offers an unforgettable way to interact with nature and experience the beauty of the area, whether you want a leisurely ride through the countryside or an adventurous exploration of the national parks.

Rock Climbing and Carving

Rock climbers and cavers will find intriguing prospects in Ronda and the surrounding area. The region offers the ideal playground for adventurers looking for vertical difficulties and subterranean investigation thanks to its rocky terrain and limestone formations.

What to expect when rock climbing and caving in and near Ronda is as follows:

Climbing rocks:

- **El Chorro:** El Chorro, a well-known rock climbing location, is about an hour's drive from Ronda. It has striking limestone cliffs, such as the famous El Caminito del Rey, which is well-known for its exhilarating via ferrata route. For climbers of all skill levels, from novices to experts, El Chorro provides a variety of routes.

- **La Cueva del Gato**: In addition to its natural beauty, La Cueva del Gato offers opportunities for rock climbing. Climbers will find difficult routes on the cave's limestone walls. After your ascent, you can cool yourself in the pool of the cave's crystal-clear water.

- **Sierra de Grazalema**: The Sierra de Grazalema Natural Park has a number of places where rock climbers can enjoy beautiful scenery. Popular crags like El Torreon and Peon Grande offer a choice of routes for climbers of all levels. While pushing yourself on the rocks in this natural park, you may take in the beautiful scenery of the area.

Caving:

- In the Sierra de Grazalema Natural Park, there is a cave

system called Cueva del Hundidero-Gato that provides an amazing caving experience. Impressive rock formations may be seen in the underground corridors and chambers, which also offer a window into the underlying environment.

Because of its complexity and potential dangers, it is recommended that you explore this cave system with an experienced guide.

- The prehistoric cave paintings of Cueva de la Pileta, which is close to the community of Benaoján, are well known. The cave also offers guided excursions that go all the way within. Along with the intriguing geological structures, stalactites, and stalagmites, you will see the old artwork.

- **Sima GESM:** The Grazalema Natural Park's Sima GESM is a vertical caving challenge for more seasoned cave divers. It is one of Andalusia's deepest and trickiest caves, requiring specialised knowledge and gear. This heart-pounding adventure plunges you deep beneath and gives you a fascinating look at the underground environment.

Prioritising safety and adhering to recommended equipment usage and rules are crucial when rock climbing and caving.

Consider hiring a local guide or attending an organised tour if you're a novice or are unfamiliar with the area to ensure a secure and pleasurable visit. Ronda offers an exhilarating playground for rock climbers and cavers alike with its various rock formations and hidden treasures.

GASTRONOMY AND LOCAL CUISINE

Traditional Andalusian Dishes

The rich flavours, brilliant colours, and fusion of various culinary influences that make up Andalusian cuisine are well-known. When you travel to Ronda, you must eat these classic Andalusian dishes:

- The traditional cold soup of Andalusia is called gazpacho. It's the ideal dish to battle the heat because it's made with ripe tomatoes, cucumbers, bell peppers, garlic, olive oil, vinegar, and bread. During the humid summer months, gazpacho is frequently served as an appetiser or light dinner.

- **Salmorejo**: A thicker variation of the chilled tomato soup, salmorejo is similar to gazpacho. Tomatoes, bread, garlic, olive oil, and sherry vinegar are used in its preparation. Diced hard-boiled eggs and cured ham are frequently added as garnishes to salmorejo to add flavour and texture.

- **Pescaito frito:** Because of Andalusia's proximity to the coast, it is a seafood haven, and the dish is a local favourite. It is made up of a selection of tiny fish, including anchovies, sardines, and baby squid, which are lightly battered and deep-fried until perfectly crispy. Enjoy the delicious flavours of the fish after adding a little lemon juice to it.

- The Spanish dish rabo de toro, which means "bull's tail," is a robust and savoury stew cooked with braised oxtail. Red wine, vegetables, garlic, and spices are slowly simmered with the meat until it is soft and easily slips off the bone. It frequently comes with a dish of rice or mashed potatoes.

- Traditional Spanish cuisine known as "migas" is cooked using day-old bread crumbs, garlic, olive oil, and optional ingredients like chorizo, bacon, or peppers. In a pan, the mixture is cooked until the bread crumbs are crispy and flavorful from the additional seasonings. Typically, migas are eaten at brunch or breakfast.

- **Tortillitas de camarones**: In Andalusia, these thin, crispy shrimp fritters are a favourite tapas dish. They are fried till golden brown using a batter made of chickpea flour, shrimp, parsley, and spices. Typically, tortillas de camarones are offered as a tasty starter or a snack.

- **Porra Antequerana:** Porra antequerana is a rich, creamy tomato soup that originates from the Andalusian town of Antequera. Although it is similar to salmorejo, the addition of bread gives it a thicker consistency.

  Green peppers, hard-boiled eggs, and diced ham are typical additions to porra antequerana.

- **Pestios**: In Andalusia, these sweet pastries are a delectable treat, especially during joyful times like Christmas. A dough consisting of flour, olive oil, sugar, and spices is fried to create pestis, which are then drizzled with honey or dusted with powdered sugar. They are eaten as a dessert or a snack and have a lovely crunch.

- **Puchero**: Puchero is a nourishing stew that is well-liked all over Andalusia. Various meats, including beef, hog, and chicken, are used in its preparation, along with chickpeas, potatoes, carrots, and cabbage.

  Slow simmering gives the stew's flavours time to mingle, creating a filling and nourishing dish.

- **Flamenquin**: A classic dish from Cordoba, an adjacent region of Andalusia, is flamenquin. Pork loin is rolled and wrapped with cured ham before being breaded and fried till crispy. It is a rich and decadent dish because of the marriage of soft pork and salty ham.

Tapas and Pintxos Culture in Ronda

Like the rest of Andalusia, Ronda has a thriving tapas culture where locals and tourists meet to eat and drink from small plates of delectable food. Here's a look at Ronda's tapas and pintxos tradition:

- **Tapas Tradition**: Free tapas are frequently provided with every drink order in taverns and restaurants in Ronda. This implies that you will get a little dish of food to eat with your beer, wine, or other beverage when you order one.

  From simple fare like olives, cheese, and cured meats to sophisticated dishes like fried fish, croquettes, or grilled veggies, tapas can take many different forms.

- **Tapas Crawl**: Participating in a "ir de tapeo," or tapas crawl, is a common method to discover Ronda's tapas scene. You can move between bars, sampling various tapas and taking in the bustling ambiance. You can sample a range of flavours because each restaurant will have its own specialty and distinctive take on classic tapas.

- Despite Ronda not having the same reputation for pintxos as the Basque Country, you can still find these delectable bite-sized delicacies in select places.

  Typically, pintxos are served on skewers or on thin pieces of bread with a variety of toppings such cured meats, shellfish, cheese, or vegetables. They are a fantastic choice for a quick snack or to go with your beverage.

- **Tapa Varieties**: The tapas in Ronda offer a mixture of fish, meats, vegetables, and regional flavours, reflecting the culinary traditions of Andalusia. Gambas al ajillo (garlic shrimp), boquerones en vinagre (marinated anchovies), tortilla espanola (Spanish omelette), albondigas (meatballs), and patatas bravas (fried potatoes with hot sauce) are a few common tapas you might come across.

  Don't forget to sample some of the regional specialties, such salmorejo and rabo de toro (bull's tail).

- In Ronda, the tapas culture is as much about mingling with others as it is about eating. It's typical to congregate with friends or family in a neighbourhood pub, chat, and take in the lively atmosphere.

Locals and visitors mix, swap tales, and enjoy the aromas of Andalusian food in the frequently convivial atmosphere.

- **Recommendations**: Some well-liked tapas establishments in Ronda area Bodega San Francisco, Tragatapas, Casa Maria, and El Lechuguita. These places are renowned for their mouthwatering tapas, welcoming staff, and traditional Andalusian ambiance.

Don't be hesitant to sample different flavours when learning about Ronda's tapas and pintxos culture. Also, ask the locals for their recommendations. It's a wonderful chance to get acquainted with Andalusian culinary customs and take in the lively social scene of this lovely city.

Wines and Wineries in the Region

Andalusia's Ronda and neighbouring areas are well recognized for their thriving wine industry and attractive wineries. Here is a look at the local wine scene and several well-known wineries:

- Ronda has a lengthy history of winemaking that dates back to the Roman era. Due to its elevation location in the Serrania de Ronda mountains, the area has a special microclimate with warm summers and cool nights. The grapevines can grow well under these circumstances.

- **Wine Types:** Ronda is well-known for its production of red wines, especially those made from the native Tintilla de Rota grape variety. Tempranillo, Cabernet Sauvignon, Syrah, and Merlot are among other prominent grape varietals grown in the area. With grapes like Pedro Ximenez and Moscatel de Alejandria, white wines are also made.

- **Wine Route:** Also known as "La Ruta del Vino de Ronda," the Ronda Wine Route is a well-liked tourism destination that lets guests experience the area's wineries, vineyards, and wine cellars. The path provides a chance to discover more about the wine-making process, sample several wines, and take in the breathtaking scenery that surrounds the vines.

Visit Wineries:

- **Bodega Descalzos Viejos**: This winery, housed in a former monastery, mixes old-world elegance with contemporary winemaking methods. They create premium red wines and provide tastings and guided tours.

- Bodega La Melonera is a winery that specialises in organic and biodynamic beverages. It is located in the charming village of Ronda. They place a strong emphasis on maintaining conventional winemaking techniques and have vineyards dispersed around the area.

- Known for its organic and ecological farming methods, Finca La Donaira is a stunning estate close to Ronda. Visitors can tour the vineyards and sample their wines, and they manufacture a variety of wines using grapes produced on their property.

- **Bodega Dona Felisa**: This family-run winery is tucked away in Ronda's breathtaking landscape. They provide guided tours, wine tastings, and the opportunity to find out more about their winemaking procedure, which uses both conventional and cutting-edge methods.

- Wine Festivals and Events: Throughout the year, Ronda conducts a number of wine festivals and events that give people the chance to celebrate and learn more about the wines produced in the area. Popular wine festivals like the Ronda Wine Festival and the Grape Harvest Festival include regional wines together with live music, food vendors, and cultural activities.

Warm hospitality, stunning scenery, and the opportunity to taste outstanding wines are all things you can look forward to when visiting Ronda's wineries. Exploring the wine and wineries of Ronda is an enriching experience that enables you to immerse yourself in the regional wine culture and appreciate the artistry that goes into each bottle, whether you're a wine connoisseur or just enjoy the beauty of vineyards.

Culinary Delights and Must-Try Restaurants

Ronda is a culinary paradise, offering a wide range of delectable dishes that highlight the flavours of Andalusia and the indigenous food in the area. Here are some Ronda eateries and gastronomic treats that you really must try:

- **Tragabuches**: This Michelin-starred establishment is renowned for its creative take on classic Andalusian fare. Modern cooking methods are combined with regional ingredients by chef Dani Garca to produce dishes that offer a distinctive dining experience. Tragabuches offers a culinary trip through Andalusian cuisine, from inventive sweets to beautifully presented fish entrees.

- **Restaurante Bardal**: Restaurante Bardal, a second

Michelin-starred establishment, specialises in modern food with a Mediterranean influence. Chef Benito Gómez uses fresh, in-season ingredients that are acquired nearby to create classic dishes with a contemporary twist. The menu presents the area's culinary traditions in a sophisticated and creative way.

- **Casa Maria**: For more than 25 years, this family-run eatery has been providing authentic Andalusian food. You may enjoy traditional meals like rabo de toro (bull's tail), grilled meats, and hearty stews at Casa Maria in a cosy and welcoming setting.

A genuine culinary experience is guaranteed by their dedication to using only the best, locally sourced ingredients.

- Almocabar is a beautiful eatery that specialises in traditional Andalusian fare and is situated in the centre of Ronda's old town. They provide a variety of foods made using fresh, local products, from tapas to whole meals. Don't overlook their amazing homemade delicacies, including the leche frita (fried milk).

- **Restaurante Almocázar:** This combination of Andalusian and foreign flavours is served in a historic structure with spectacular views of the Puente Nuevo.

Their menu offers inventive recipes made with regional ingredients that are suitable for both vegetarians and meat eaters. Dining in a romantic environment while enjoying sweeping views of Ronda is possible on the rooftop terrace.

- De Locos Tapas is a well-known restaurant that displays Ronda's thriving tapas tradition for a more relaxed dining experience.

  They provide a wide range of tapas, including both classic classics and innovative, tasty takes on old favourites. With your tapas, sip some regional wine or a cool sangria.

- **Restaurante Pedro Romero**: Named for the renowned bullfighter from Ronda, Restaurante Pedro Romero serves a variety of Andalusian dishes, both traditional and modern. The eatery serves salmorejo, grilled meats, and fresh seafood while paying respect to the region's bullfighting history. A great lunch can be enjoyed in the stylish atmosphere of the dining room.

- **El Lechuguita**: This inviting and well-liked tapas bar is renowned for its ample portions and welcoming ambiance. There are many different tapas options available at El Lechuguita, including their renowned montaditos (little sandwiches) that are stuffed with tasty ingredients like cheese, jamón ibérico, and marinated fish.
  It's a terrific place to meet locals and take in Ronda's bustling tapas culture.

- When eating out in Ronda, make sure to sample some of the regional specialties, such rabo de toro, gazpacho, and local wines, which are made to go wonderfully with the cuisine of the area. You will certainly have a great and enjoyable eating experience thanks to Ronda's culinary marvels.

DAY TRIPS FROM RONDA

Exploring the White Villages (Pueblos Blancos)

In the area surrounding Ronda, visiting the White Villages, or Pueblos Blancos, is an interesting and beautiful experience.

These little towns are distinguished by their whitewashed homes, winding lanes, and stunning hilltop settings. A list of some of the top Pueblos Blancos near Ronda is provided below:

- Setenil de las Bodegas is a distinctive community distinguished by its homes carved out of the surrounding cliffs and rock formations. As you stroll through the streets, you'll be astounded by the houses that have been carved out of the rocks, producing an amazing architectural spectacle. Also offering breathtaking views of the surrounding area is Setenil de las Bodegas.

- **Zahara de la Sierra:** Zahara de la Sierra, perched on a mountain overlooking a lovely lake, offers breathtaking all-encompassing views. Discover the village's winding streets, tour the abandoned castle from the Middle Ages, and take in the peace. Hiking trails and water sports are available at the neighbouring reservoir.

- **Grazalema**: This village is a haven for those who enjoy the outdoors because it is encircled by the Sierra de Grazalema Natural Park. Explore the picturesque alleys lined with white buildings and flower-filled balconies, go hiking or birdwatching in the park, and breathe in the clean mountain air. Grazalema is renowned for its handmade crafts and traditional woolen blankets.

- **Arcos de la Frontera:** Arcos de la Frontera, perched atop a rocky slope, provides breathtaking views of the Guadalupe River Valley. Its old district is a maze of winding lanes, arches, and whitewashed homes decorated with vibrant flowers. The magnificent Santa Maria Basilica and the Castle of Arcos are not to be missed.

- **Olvera**: Another treasure of the Pueblos Blancos, Olvera is crowned by a magnificent Moorish castle. San Juan de Letrán, the village's lovely church, and the eye-catching white buildings that flow down the hillside are its most notable features. Take a stroll down the Calle Llana, which is dotted with quaint restaurants and boutiques.

- **Casares**: Casares, which is perched atop a precipitous hill, offers stunning views of both the Mediterranean Sea and the Sierra Bermeja mountains. The village's attractive squares, winding streets, and ancient castle remains are its defining features. It's the ideal location to take in the peace and allure of a typical Andalusian village.

- Even though it's not exactly a Pueblos Blancos hamlet, Mijas is a beautiful white community that's worth visiting. On the Costa del Sol, the town of Mijas provides a distinctive fusion of coastal beauty and old-world Andalusian charm. Visit the bullring, stroll through the winding lanes, and take in the expansive views from the Mirador de la Muralla.

Take your time when touring the Pueblos Blancos so you may meander through the streets, take in the neighbourhood vibe, and find secret nooks. Each village offers a look into the rich cultural legacy of the area and has its distinct personality. Don't forget to sample the cuisine, look around at the crafts, and take in the beauty of these charming white villages.

Visiting the Ancient City of Acinipo

A fascinating journey into the past can be had by visiting the historic city of Acinipo. Acinipo, a significant Roman hamlet about 20 kilometres from Ronda, provides a look into the area's rich history and archaeological legacy. The following is a guide to touring the historic city of Acinipo:

- **History of Acinipo**: In the first century AD, the Romans founded Acinipo, also known as "Ronda la Vieja" (Old Ronda). It was known for producing wine and olive oil and was a thriving city with a sizable population. The inhabitants slowly shifted to the area that is now Ronda as Acinipo lost prominence throughout time.

- Site: You can explore the remains of this ancient city at the Acinipo archaeological site. The site's showpiece, a well-preserved Roman theatre, can be found after exploring the remains. The theatre still has its original orchestra, stage, and seating tiers, giving visitors a glimpse of its former splendour.

- **Acinipo** is situated on a hilltop and provides panoramic views of the surrounding area. Spend a moment admiring the breathtaking views, which include the Sierra de las Nieves mountains and the verdant lowlands. The appeal of this historic city is enhanced by its natural beauty.

- Visit the Interpretive Center, which is next to the entrance, before you go to the site. You can learn more about the background and significance of Acinipo here through the exhibitions, artefacts, and explanations that are provided. Your knowledge of the significance of the site from an archaeological standpoint is improved by the centre's insightful context.

- Consider taking a guided tour of Acinipo to learn more about the significance and history of the historic city. The ruins can be brought to life with the help of experts who can offer fascinating tales and give in-depth explanations about the remains.

- **Plan Your Visit**: Because Acinipo is an outdoor location, careful planning is required. For walking, put on some comfortable shoes because the ground could be uneven. Bring water, sunscreen, and a hat, particularly in the summer when it's hot. It's also a good idea to research the site's opening times and any tourist restrictions beforehand.

The opportunity to travel back in time and fully appreciate the architectural and historical legacy of the Romans is provided by a visit to the ancient city of Acinipo.

The theatre is in excellent condition, and the nearby ruins offer a fascinating look at the prehistoric culture that formerly flourished here. If you want to get the most out of your investigation of the area's rich historical and cultural legacy, combine your visit to Acinipo with a trip to Ronda.

Discovering Grazalema Natural Park

Nature lovers and outdoor adventurers will truly enjoy exploring Grazalema Natural Park. This protected region, which is a portion of the Sierra de Grazalema mountain range and is situated in the province of Cádiz, is well-known for its breathtaking scenery, varied flora and fauna, and outdoor activities.

To help you get the most out of your trip to Grazalema Natural Park, here is a guide:

- Grazalema Natural Park is a hiker's paradise, offering a variety of paths that are suitable for walkers of all ability levels. On scenic treks, discover the park's stunning woodlands, limestone peaks, and river valleys. Popular paths include the Garganta Verde Trail, which leads to an impressive gorge, and the Pinsapar Trail, where you can see the uncommon Spanish fir trees. Before beginning your hike, don't forget to check the park's rules and get any necessary permits.

- **Wildlife and birdwatching**: A wide range of animals, including the endangered Spanish Ibex, wild boars, and several bird species, can be found in the park. The chance to see spectacular raptors like the Golden Eagle and Griffon vulture will excite birdwatchers. As you explore the park, bring your binoculars and keep a lookout for these intriguing creatures.

- **Towns & Cultural Heritage**: The gorgeous white Pueblos Blancos towns, which dot the Grazalema Natural Park, are each endowed with a certain charm.

Visit the village bearing the same name, Grazalema, and stroll through its winding alleyways lined with whitewashed homes.

Explore Benamahoma, a quaint village tucked away in the middle of the park, or Zahara de la Sierra, with its magnificent castle and panoramic vistas. Enjoy the warm welcome of the locals while immersing yourself in the culture and visiting historical locations.

- **Caving and canyoning:** Grazalema Natural Park provides caving and canyoning chances for people looking for adventure. In the company of experts, explore the park's limestone caverns to learn more about its subterranean environment. Explore deep canyons, make your way through gorges, and test your mettle with exhilarating water rappelling adventures. These activities offer a distinctive viewpoint on the geology and natural formations of the park.

- **Natural Pools and Waterfalls:** During the hotter months, take a refreshing dip in one of the park's many natural pools or waterfalls. Swim in the cool, clear water and take in the quiet of the area. The Charco del Canalón natural pool and the Salto del Cabrero waterfall are two well-known locations.

- **Local cuisine:** Indulge in the mouth watering fare of the area after a day of exploration. Try up some classic fare including substantial stews, grilled meats, and regional cheeses. The lovely cafes and restaurants in the park's villages let you sample the cuisine of Andalusia.

Remember to respect the environment, stay on authorised pathways, and follow any rules or regulations established by the park administration when visiting Grazalema Natural Park.

Spend some time admiring the park's beauty, taking in the crisp mountain air, and letting yourself get lost in the peace of this natural haven.

Venturing to the Coastal Towns of Andalusia

Going to the Andalusia coastal cities gives a wonderful combination of sun, sea, and colourful Spanish culture. The region's coastal towns provide something for everyone, from bustling beach resorts to charming fishing villages. The following locations on the Andalusian coast are a must-see:

- **Costa del Sol**: Also referred to as the "Sun Coast," the Costa del Sol is a well-liked vacation spot featuring a variety of seaside cities and resorts. With its posh beach clubs and expensive stores, Marbella offers luxury and glitz.

  While Nerja is well known for its beautiful coves like Burriana Beach and the well-known Balcony of Europe, Fuengirola is known for its long, sandy beaches and a bustling promenade.

- **Cadiz**: This ancient port city on the Atlantic coast is renowned for its stunning beaches and rich nautical heritage.

  Visit the Cadiz Cathedral, stroll through the old town's meandering alleyways, and unwind in one of the city's many tapas bars. La Caleta Beach, renowned for its picturesque location between two castles, should not be missed.

- At the southernmost point of continental Europe, Tarifa is known for its powerful winds and is a sanctuary for fans of windsurfing and kitesurfing. With its winding alleyways, hopping markets, and picturesque old town, the town exudes a bohemian air. The beach at Playa de Los

Lances is well-liked for water sports and tanning.

- Malaga, the biggest city on the Costa del Sol, is home to a variety of historical, cultural, and beachside attractions. Visit the Alcazaba fortress, explore the Picasso Museum, and stroll along La Malagueta Beach's lively promenade. Malaga is renowned for its mouthwatering seafood and exciting nightlife.

- Almeria is a city with a remarkable Moorish past that is located on the southeast coast of Andalusia. Visit the Alcazaba, a massive stronghold that commands a view of the city, and stroll around the old town to see the distinctive white residences. In close proximity, in the Cabo de Gata-Nijar Natural Park, you may see pristine beaches, towering cliffs, and unusual plants and animals.

- **Huelva**: A coastal community with a lengthy maritime history, Huelva is tucked between the Guadalquivir River and the Atlantic Ocean. Visit the Christopher Columbus Monument, stroll through the city's historic district, and take in the stunning Punta Umbrella and Mazagón beaches. Fresh seafood is another specialty of Huelva, particularly the city's well-known gambas blancas (white prawns).

- **Estepona**: A lovely town famed for its typical Andalusian architecture and picturesque old town, Estepona is situated between Marbella and Gibraltar. Visit the Orchid House, a distinctive botanical garden, and stroll along its lovely promenade while taking in the golden sand beaches.

The coastal cities of Andalusia offer a wide variety of experiences, whether you're looking to unwind on the beach, indulge in delectable cuisine, or immerse yourself in history and culture.

Discover the distinctive appeal of each seaside jewel along the Andalusian coastline, take in the colourful atmosphere, and enjoy the Mediterranean climate.

PRACTICAL INFORMATION AND RESOURCES

Currency, Language, and Communication
Transportation in and around Ronda

- **Currency**: The Euro (€) is Spain's official unit of exchange. It is widely accepted throughout Ronda, and you may convert money at any bank, exchange bureau, or ATM. Additionally, most major credit cards are accepted.

- **Language**: Spanish is the major tongue used in Ronda and throughout the rest of Spain. However, because it is a well-known tourist destination, you can frequently come across

English-speaking locals there, particularly in hotels, eateries, and tourist attractions.

- **Communication**: Internet connectivity and dependable mobile phone coverage are available in Ronda. For your mobile phone, you can buy prepaid SIM cards or use international roaming services; the majority of hotels, cafes, and restaurants have free Wi-Fi.

Ronda's surrounding areas' transportation:

- **Walking**: Ronda is a small city that is simple to navigate on foot. The old district of the city is pedestrian-friendly, and many of the sights, eateries, and stores are close by.

- **Public transportation:** Ronda's local bus service connects the many city neighbourhoods. You may get schedules and ticket details online or at the bus station, which is close to the city centre. Buses are a practical means of getting to neighbouring towns and villages.

- **Taxis**: You may easily locate taxis in Ronda at authorised taxi stands or by phoning for a pickup. Taxis can be a practical means of transportation when travelling small distances or with luggage.

- **Rental cars**: In Ronda, you can rent a car if you'd like more freedom and flexibility. You can reserve a car in advance or when you arrive at the city's offices of several car rental companies. Because Ronda is well-connected by roadways, having a car lets you see the region at your own time.

- **Train**: A few kilometres from the city centre, Ronda has a train station. Ronda is connected by train to important towns including Malaga, Seville, and Madrid. Longer distances can be covered in comfort and beauty by train.

Planning ahead for your transportation requirements is a good idea, especially if you're visiting during a busy tourist season. To make the most of your time in and around Ronda, weigh the convenience, cost, and distance of various kinds of transportation.

Safety Tips and Emergency Contacts

When travelling, safety is always the top consideration. Following are some safety recommendations and emergency numbers to have in mind while visiting Ronda:

Tips for general safety

- Be mindful of your surroundings and believe in your gut.
- Keep your possessions safe, and refrain from flaunting pricey stuff in public.
- Keep to populated, well-lit locations, particularly at night.
- Use safe modes of transportation, and use authorised taxis.
- Respect local culture and adhere to local laws and customs.

Emergency numbers:

- Police: Dial 112 to contact the police in case of an emergency or to report a crime.
- Medical Emergencies: Call 112 to request an ambulance or visit the emergency room of the closest hospital.
- Fire Department: Dial 112 to contact the fire department in the event of a fire or other related emergency.

Safety and Health:

- Invest in travel insurance that includes emergency and medical coverage.
- Make sure you know where the nearest pharmacy and medical facilities are.
- Keep yourself hydrated, especially during the hot summer months, and avoid getting too much sun.

- Be mindful of any allergies or dietary restrictions, and abide by the rules on the safety of your food and drink.
- Keep any necessary drugs on hand and in their original containers with the appropriate labelling.

Local laws and ordinances

- Learn about Spain's local laws and ordinances, such as the prohibitions on public smoking, alcohol drinking, and traffic regulations.
- Carry the relevant identification, such as a copy of your passport.

Information and Communication:

- Keep crucial contact information, such as the phone number and address of your embassy or consulate, close to hand.

- Keep yourself up to date on any travel advisories, local weather forecasts, and news events that could affect your safety.
- Keeping in mind that these are general safety recommendations, it is always important to travel with caution and common sense. Although Ronda is generally regarded as a safe place to visit, it is still advisable to be cautious of your surroundings and take the required safety steps to guarantee a hassle-free and pleasurable trip.

Useful Websites and Apps

There are a number of helpful websites and apps that can improve your trip to Ronda and offer helpful information. Here are a few suggestions:

Websites:

- Official Ronda Tourism Website: The official Ronda tourism website offers in-depth details about the city's attractions, events, lodgings, and useful travel advice. To learn more, go to www.rondatourism.com.

- TripAdvisor is a well-known travel site that provides opinions, rankings, and suggestions for Ronda hotels, restaurants, sites, and activities. You can use it to organise your travels and make wise judgments. Please go to www.tripadvisor.com.

- **Google Maps**: Google Maps is a great resource for getting around Ronda and for navigating. It offers thorough maps, instructions, and up-to-date traffic information. Additionally, you may look up neighbouring eateries, sights to see, and other areas of interest. Visit www.google.com/maps to access it.

- Skyscanner is a helpful website for comparing rates and locating the cheapest travel bargains if you're still in the process of organising your vacation and need to locate flights to Ronda. Visit the SkyScanner website.

Apps:

- Google Maps (App): The Google Maps app is essential for getting around Ronda and exploring the area. It offers offline maps, real-time traffic updates, and turn-by-turn directions. accessible on iOS and Android.

- The Ronda-specific travel app Ronda - Travel Guide & Offline Map provides offline maps, in-depth details about sights, restaurants, and hotels, as well as insider advice and recommendations. accessible on iOS.

- **XE Currency (App):** You can easily convert currencies and keep track of exchange rates with the help of this dependable currency converter app. It helps you keep track of your spending and exchange rates. accessible on iOS and Android.

- **Spanish Translator (App):** If you don't speak Spanish, having a translator app on your phone can be useful. Spanish Translator offers translations for frequent expressions and terms to facilitate communication with native speakers. accessible on iOS and Android.

To guarantee you have access to any important apps and maps when offline or without an internet connection, don't forget to download them before your journey.

These online resources and mobile applications can help you plan your trip, get around town, identify the finest places to stay and eat, and generally improve your travel experience in Ronda.

Essential Useful Phrases

Communication with locals can be made much easier and your vacation experience can be much improved by learning a few simple words in the language. Here are some key words and phrases in Spanish that you should know before visiting Ronda:

Greetings and Basic Expressions:

- Hello: Hola
- Good morning: Buenos días
- Good afternoon: Buenas tardes
- Good evening: Buenas noches
- Please: Por favor
- Thank you: Gracias
- You're welcome: De nada
- Excuse me: Perdón/Disculpe

Introductions and Socialising:

- My name is...: Me llamo...

- What is your name?: ¿Cómo te llamas? (informal) / ¿Cómo se llama? (formal)
- Nice to meet you: Mucho gusto
- How are you?: ¿Cómo estás? (informal) / ¿Cómo está? (formal)
- I'm fine, thank you: Estoy bien, gracias
- Where are you from?: ¿De dónde eres? (informal) / ¿De dónde es usted? (formal)

Directions and Transportation:

- Where is...?: ¿Dónde está...?
- How do I get to...?: ¿Cómo llego a...?
- Is it far?: ¿Está lejos?
- Left: Izquierda
- Right: Derecha
- Straight ahead: Todo recto
- Bus station: Estación de autobuses
- Train station: Estación de tren

Ordering Food and Drinks:

- I would like...: Me gustaría...
- What do you recommend?: ¿Qué me recomienda?
- Do you have a menu in English?: ¿Tiene un menú en inglés?
- Water: Agua
- Beer: Cerveza
- Wine: Vino
- Coffee: Café
- Bill, please: La cuenta, por favor

Emergency Situations:

- Help!: ¡Ayuda!
- I need a doctor: Necesito un médico
- Where's the nearest hospital?: ¿Dónde está el hospital más cercano?
- I lost my bag: He perdido mi bolso
- I need to call the police: Necesito llamar a la policía

Remember that learning a few simple Spanish words will be welcomed by the locals and can improve your interactions and experiences while visiting Ronda.

CONCLUSION

In conclusion, Ronda is a fascinating location that offers a rich fusion of culinary, history, and culture. With the help of this thorough travel manual, you'll have all the knowledge you need to enjoy your trip to Ronda in 2023.

You gained knowledge of Ronda's alluring beauty and the benefits of going there in the upcoming year. The guide offered insightful advice on how to use the book successfully, the ideal time to visit, how to get to Ronda, what is needed for a visa, and where to stay.

To ensure a pleasant and secure flight, you looked into important travel advice, safety considerations, and emergency contacts. You may fully immerse yourself in Ronda's history by reading about the city's interesting past as well as its historical sites, museums, and art galleries in the book.

You also learned about Ronda's top sights, such as the famous Puente Nuevo, the Bullring, the Old Town, the Arab Baths, and the lovely Alameda del Tajo gardens. You also gained knowledge of outdoor pursuits including hiking, trail running, and exploring the Sierra de las Nieves Natural Park.

The tour exposed you to traditional Andalusian foods, tapas and pintxos culture, local wine and wineries, as well as suggested eateries and gastronomic pleasures, to fulfil your appetite.

Additionally, you learned about surrounding places like the Andalusia seaside villages, the White Villages, the old city of Acinipo, and Grazalema Natural Park. Additionally, the guide included details on vital topics including money, languages, travel, and websites and apps.

You'll be able to speak with people more efficiently and get around Ronda more easily if you become familiar with some basic Spanish words.

With this travel manual in your possession, you are prepared to visit Ronda in 2023 and have a very unique experience. Discover this charming city's charm, take in its eye-catching attractions, indulge in its delectable cuisine, and make lifelong memories there. Have fun on your trip to Ronda!

Fond Farewell to Ronda

It's time to say a heartfelt goodbye to this magical city as your time in Ronda draws to a close. Your vacation experience has been forever changed by Ronda, whether it was because you visited its ancient sites, took in the breath-taking views, or savoured its delectable cuisine.

Think back on the experiences you've had, the relationships you've formed with the people there, and the natural beauty you've seen. You have undoubtedly fallen in love with Ronda because of its fascinating history, beautiful scenery, and welcoming people.

Remember to bring the tales and experiences that have developed during your stay with you as you depart. Your voyage will always include the relationships you made, the cultural exchanges you had, and the moments you were in amazement and wonder.

The memories and the spirit of Ronda will stay with you even if you may be physically leaving the city. Keep in mind the knowledge gained, the respect for various cultures, and the spirit of adventure that Ronda has ingrained in you.

Let Ronda's allure motivate you to carry on your voyage of discovery and travel, whether you have plans to go back someday or visit new locations. As you set out for new horizons, embrace your inner nomad and keep Ronda close to your heart.

Ronda, I'll miss you until our next encounter. We are grateful for the beautiful memories and experiences you have shared. Wishing you joy, exploration, and the same magic that Ronda has brought into your life on your journeys in the future. Have a safe trip, and may your trips surpass your experiences in Ronda.

Making Lasting Memories

Making enduring memories is an essential component of every travel experience, and your time in Ronda undoubtedly gave you plenty of chances to do so. Here are some ideas for how to create enduring memories while you're there:

- **Embrace the Present**: Focus on the beauty and originality of your surroundings by being totally present in each moment. Spend some time taking in Ronda's sights, sounds, and fragrances. To fully immerse yourself in the event, use all of your senses.

- **Interact with Locals**: Talk to the locals, listen to their experiences, and develop an understanding of their way of life. Making ties with the neighbourhood can help you have a better grasp of the culture there.

- **Try Something New**: Step outside your comfort zone and engage in Ronda-specific activities or experiences. Pushing your limits can result in lifelong experiences, whether it's participating in a local festival, attempting traditional cuisine, or taking part in adventure sports.

- **Capture the Moments:** Before snapping a snapshot, take some time to really appreciate the moment. You may thoroughly enjoy the experience and have concrete recollections to look back on by juggling the act of recording memories with being present in them.

- Keeping a journal or writing a trip diary will allow you to document your experiences, ideas, and feelings. Recording your thoughts, comments, and daily highlights will help you keep the memories alive and give you a way to revisit your journey in the future.

- **Participate in Local Traditions**: Get a feel for the community by taking part in local customs or going to festivals and events. By participating in the local traditions and rituals, you'll make special memories and develop a greater understanding of the culture.

- **Reflect and Share:** Take the time to consider your experiences, tell loved ones about them, or even start a travel blog to chronicle your travels. By telling people about your travels, you can relive the moments and encourage them to set out on their own travel adventures.

Keep in mind that the real worth of travel is found not only in the destinations you visit, but also in the encounters and memories you make along the route. Indulge in Ronda's magic, cherish the moments, and enjoy the satisfaction of creating priceless memories that you will cherish long after you leave this alluring city.

Printed in Great Britain
by Amazon

44874061R00096